Narrow]

With Margin

Poems by Boltini

Published by Otley Word Feast Press 2015
OWF Press Community Interest Company
9B Westgate, Otley, West Yorkshire, LS21 3AT

ISBN 978-0-9927616-4-6

Printed by
imprintdigital.com, Seychelles Farm, Upton Pyne, Devon
EX5 5YX
info@imprintdigital.com

To Colin Wood, the English teacher who found time to offer encouragement and friendship to a bewildered pupil more than 50 years ago. And to all great teachers.

Acknowledgements

Most of all I must thank Jane Kite. Without Jane's patience and perseverance these poems would have remained in longhand in chaotic bundles of A4 (narrow ruled feint with margin my preference). Also, I'd like to thank Sandra Burnett of Otley Word Feast Press for her help and support, and all the Otley Poets for sharing the thrills and spills of our work and wordplay over these many years.

Boltini
May 2015

Introduction

Tony Boltini has always fascinated and amazed me in performance – and made me laugh and laugh and laugh. So it's great that Otley Word Feast Press are publishing his first collection of poetry. And what a feast it is!

I hadn't clocked how well Boltini knows his animals until I read through this full manuscript. He inhabits them, illuminates them, feels their lives and their tragedies, and becomes them in ways I've not known in any other poet. Everything from the falcon who wants to open a delicatessen, through Ozymandias the cockerel; a wonderfully befuddled yet canny bear; Champion the Wonder Horse; assassin anteaters, and on to a lay preacher sparrow. Each captured in all their barmy and life-enhancing glory by Boltini's daft rhyme schemes, and his eye for the absurd.

But this isn't just a brilliant zoo of a book, Boltini manages to winkle out all sorts of human frailties and eccentricities, not just through his animals, but also through poignant poems about the demon drink and bawdy poems about struggling with hard-ons in church. He laces many of his poems with what is clearly a lot of knowledge, and years of thought, about the strangeness of religious faith – and deals with what could be a heavy subject with a skilled lightness of touch.

If you haven't yet seen Boltini in performance – get along to one of his gigs instantly! You will – I guarantee – be blown away. Revel in Tony's superb Lancashire burr, the richness of his voice, his perfect comic timing, and the way he lulls you into security and then gives you a rabbit punch with sudden no-holds-barred poems like For Shirley, Lost Boy or Corbies.

Enjoy Boltini – on stage and on the page. If you don't laugh or get a lump in your throat, with any of these poems, you need to check you've still got a pulse.

Char March
April 2015

CONTENTS

Do one thing for me, Sredni Vashtar.

Saki

In the Beginning

Early March, the ice is gone
though a bitter wind yet stirs
the surface of the pond;
frogs wake up.

The girls are pretty as snowdrops.
Oh how the boys desire them.

Of what have frogs been dreaming
all through their winter's drowse?
Of pussy willows, catkins,
the trembling wren

or of this moment now,
lubriciously embroiled,
churning in spawn
at the edge of the pond.

The girls are pretty as snowdrops.
Oh how the boys desire them.

The Investigative Journalist

I would like to have a go at crochet, bemoaned the buffalo,
*needlepoint, quilting, embroidery – but how can I
with these great horny hooves?*

Aeronautics, said the crayfish.

Oh I do so agree, space exploration, said the hippo,
*the further the better to boldly go, that would do me.
Blast-off!* Then he gave a big belch, then he said sorry.

Puccini, said the guinea-fowl, *I would sing opera.
To dance,* said the python from flat on his belly,
the New York Met. Passion. Drama. Give me ballet.

A career in nursing, said the porcupine,
*'s not so easy when you're covered in spines.
But where's Wren? He's next isn't he?
He'll be banging on as usual I expect
about investigative journalism.
Not here? Well he might have an assignment.
Never mind. Carry on.*

Comedy, said the lion,
it's the way I tell 'em. Did you hear the one about –
Next! said the porcupine.

Disco, said the flea,
*Hip-Hop, Blue-Grass, R and B
Oh I got rhythm. I'd be a D.J. me.*

Banking, said the tuna, *in commerce immerse me.
I'd be devilish rich and all-around the world.
I'd swim in a pink Ferrari.*

*My talons would be an impediment
in any other line of work,* grumbled the falcon.
*I could never, for instance, open a delicatessen.
Mmmmm... anchovies.*

The baboon felt drawn to tourism.
I would lead small exclusive groups

around sites of great antiquity, he said.
The only thing that worries me's my appetite
for self-abuse and sodomy. Do you think it would put people off?

A louse from high on the neck of a giraffe said, *If*
I had a combined degree in architecture and engineering
I could explore the further possibilities of ferro-concrete
structures,
towers and bridges specially, but being as it is...

And all the while the Great Designer watched.

Then as he watched the creatures began to melt away.
They withdrew when they heard the footfall,
caught the scent of a man approaching and he,
the all-time champion record-breaking malcontent
was saying:

> *I want. I want. I want. I want.*
> *I want every answer.*
> *I want to live for ever.*
> *I want fame.*
> *I want wealth.*
> *I want a bigger dick and more of it.*
> *I want women.*
> *I want power... I deserve it.*
> *A bigger better faster sexier planet*
> *I want...*
> > *oh good grief is that the time?*
> > *I've got to get home to feed the cat.*

The Great Designer smiled.

And the cat in the sunshine yawned and stretched.
She was feeling rather pleased.
She said, *Well, I would never complain about my lot*
but that servant of mine – would you happen to know –
is he on his way with the food yet?

The Great Designer smiled once again
and the cat – very very slyly when no-one was looking –
went *spTHh , spTHh, spTHh, spTHh*
and the feathers she spat out were the feathers of a wren.

3

Aunty Mary

Ants in an anthill,
Aunty Mary's very ill.

Bats in a belfry,
both her lungs are shot to hell.

Cats curl up beside the fire,
Aunty Mary gasps for air.

A final groan,
the crows fly home.

Boy scouts meeting in a shed,
Aunty Mary cold and dead.

Grey life lost, nothing found,
Spinster Mary underground.

Hammer and chisel, tap-tap-tap,
Simple Bill will carve the marble.

Carve a heart, carve a dove,
shed a tear, tap-tap-tap,

Simple Bill.
Simple Bill never spoke his love.

After the Fattening

Little Lamb, Little Lamb,
if you'd grow to be ewe or ram
take this hint now please and scram.

Rosemary is the farmer's wife,
she goes into the garden.

The farmer's wife is picking mint,
the farmer's sick of Spam.

He licks his lips,
he hones his knife, he calls –

*Here, Little Lamb, my precious Little Lamb,
my tender, cherished, hand-reared orphan.
Here now... Here now... Come.*

Magellan

Accounts as they say may vary,
but Magellan I believe was only a toddler
when his father, a rude farmer said:

> *Hey, how many times do I have to tell you?*
> *Keep away from the duck pond son,*
> *it's fucking deep. If you fall in you'll drown,*
> *here, let this be a reminder*

and he gave the lad the benefit of a meaty slap
to the side of his head.

Born a rebel, Magellan took against his old man,
against his vicious determination to wring a profit
from the land regardless of cost or decency.

Magellan aged sixteen, had he been aware of Greek drama,
would have had his father's head boiled alive and eaten some,
just for the pleasure of hearing his work described by the chorus.

Instead, what he did was, he left home,
and to avenge his mother, who all her life
had to work like a slave milking goats
and sleeping always on the drafty side of the bed,
he set out to explore the vast uncharted oceans of the world.

And with what formidable success! Undreamed of feats
for a man who all his life harboured a fear of ducks.
Ducks erupting in his sleep, the ducks
he must confront and vanquish in a bloodbath nightly
of mangled beaks, webbed feet and feathers,
the hellish quacking.

Undreamed of feats for a man whose ardent member –
so rejected lovers would attest –
was no great towering main-mast
and of less than average girth.

Magellan, a man to command fleets.
Magellan, a man to kindle in our quailing hearts the spark
that might inspire us to wrestle down the demons,
the claws, the hooks, the thorns, the ducks
that would impede us.

Come All Ye

i   *Faith*

I'm a cow
yes I know
I am here
on God's pasture

I'm a placid animal
an ungulate
no high I.Q.
I'm normal

I lactate
I moo
regurgitate my cud
and chew

what more Lord
would you have me do
gain circus skills
jump through hoops

while I wait for the farmer to come
our farmer will come
to gather us in
he will open the gate

ii   *A Greater Pond*

I look you in the eye
I'm the right one for me
I am what I should be
        a Frog   Yup
        a Frog   Yup

I hop plop into the pond
croak in chorus   spawn in spring
for Frogs   Yup   the perfect thing
to be as we are
and I am as I am
land or water

Yup   an amphibian
Yup   an amphibian
and nothing escapes my bulging eye

I watch and I watch
I watch go by the tench and moorhen
damselfly dragonfly caddis fly larvae
gnats and newts water boatmen

and I wonder Yup   I wonder Yup
at such diversity   what's it for
why isn't everything froggy like me

or sometimes on a summer's eve
I may be afloat on a favourite log
I'm comfy with a bellyful drowsily contented

when with no warning a thought might come
            to stab me like a heron Yup
            it stabs me like a heron Yup
this doubt   a question

could it be I miss something
could there be anything beyond our bog
some mighty swamp   a greater pond

            one great leap   Yup
            one great leap   Yup
one great leap beyond

iii   *Beast of Burden*

if you are broken-winded sag-backed
over-laden grey dusty beaten,

if over your shoulders you wear a black cross
from the time, they say, you once carried Jesus,

if you hobble to a painful standstill,
tilt one limp defeated ear towards the preacher:

            ...evil ways... roads to damnation...
            gardens of paradise... paths to salvation...

9

if you listen, if you allow
there is more to all this than chance and chaos

then you are an Ass and you will eat thistles
Eee-Haw Eeee-haw Eee-haaaw.

iv   *In the Grass*

Bad press,
we never had a chance
right from the start in Genesis.

An ancestor
implicated the word says,
in some disobedience.

Arrant nonsense,
kangaroo court, vested interests,
no independent witness

and we are deemed guilty ever since:
originally sinuous,
serpents.

But forgive and forget shall we?
Let's be friends. Come close. Closer.
Yes that's nice, stroke me.

Now, do tell,
you can say it in a whisper
no one will hear –

What do you like the very best of all?
Tender fruit?
Trust me.

v   *In Her Own Image*

Well now you are here, said the cat,
deigning to open one eye very slightly,
and since you presume to ask I will tell you:

*God is slinky like me. She lolls in the sun
on the tombs of pharaohs, is luxurious, has claws,
is benign of countenance. Generally.*

*God does not like mice. She might, on a whim,
go wildcat scat, doolally-frantic,
climb a tree.*

She approves always –
                DON'T DO THAT
 – of the greater tranquility.

*God is not to be trifled with.
Displeasure has no part in it when you are a God.
Annoyance –*
                DON'T I SAID
– annoyance will not be tolerated

 *because God when provoked, if she chooses,
can in an instant become a hissing spitting vengeful fury,
rake out an eye, unzip a belly,*

*but ordinarily, God, like me, prefers stealth.
She may move after dark in mysterious ways.
She knows the will of the world is to please her.*

And now, said the cat, *it's getting rather hot.
Must I move, where's the shade?*
A convenient cloud obscures the sun.

And no more questions, the cat said testily.
*It's becoming tiresome. Your time is up.
You have been warned.*
                DON'T
*Oh you shouldn't have done that,
stand well back,
God's tail is twitching.*

11

vi Ozymandias

1 Alive

Cock-a-Doodle-Doooooo… Pay Attention.
Rather splendid what! Is everybody watching?
Time for a strut.

Sunlight, playing on the plumes of my tail, is it?
Colours of every conceivable burnished hue,
coruscating are they, down across my mantle?
Can everybody see?

Oh I must, I just can't help it,
chest out, wings flapping, head flung back, –O YES,
Cock-a-Doodle-Doooooo I crow

to draw your attention to
how dazzling I am. How resplendent,
omnipotent, omniscient, a truly magnificent
Cock of the Farmyard Midden.

The hens down there, all mine,
my cock-a-doodle harem.
I like it when they run away
so I can chase them. And nab one.
Or two. And I cock-a-doodle-do.

And the bantams?
Well, if the fancy takes me, yes I'm boss.
And actually I should be higher, don't you think?
I should be top of the church spire
so the whole parish might see my glory

and reaffirm how very right it is, and proper,
this pecking order of things
that crowns me Farmyard Birdbrain King.

For it is all, as you know, thanks to me;
my crowing summons morning,
my calls bring forth the sun
and the hand that follows comes in obedience
to scatter our golden corn.

2 *Dead*

The wife called him Ozymandias.
He'd had his day.

(The farmyard flock's got a new cock now.
A young 'un, what a dandy.
Fresh blood, good for the progeny.)

And tough was he, I can tell you, leather boot,
but us old farmers we won't waste 'owt;
hung for a week and simmered all night
he made a tangy stock.

And laugh? You should've been here,
the old blaggard got such a shock:
squawks of *Treason. Outrage. Blue Murder,*
with his neck laid out on the chopping block.

One last grand tour, without a crown,
he staggered round his old domain.

vii *Velvet Underground*

Go, you missionaries,
leave our pilgrim tunnels,
leave our runs uncluttered by your wayside votive shrines.

Take your tired metaphors.
What for this light you would have us see?
No cowled or shrouded monks you'll make of us
or solitary priests to feed your zeal.

Away with your parables.
Leave us our godless velvet dark
where the whispering roots instruct us;
they make no mention of ancient martyrs
or for that matter, collection boxes.

Crunching worms is wrong you say,
our molehills a sin. Enough. Be gone.
No more talk of Heavenly Pastures,
Almighty Lawns and Swards above.

dzzzzzzz…
zzzzaaahhh don't call me fly
I'm more than that
I'm deadly
                    tsetse - tsetse

you kill me
as I bite you
and that's not
etsi - getsi

you get fever
then you die
don't fret
why worry

it can't be helped
there is no God
it's just your
destineeeeee
                    tsetse - tsetse
                    tsetse - tsetse

Ye Gods

All these years I've been waiting, nursing the hurt.
They lied to us when we were children. They said,
The time will come when everyone will know the name of
Champion, The Wonder Horse.

But if you care to pose the question, and you must,
even educated well-dressed people in the street
will say, *No, I'm sorry. Can't help you there I'm afraid,*
Champion the who?

So, that promised day, what happened?
It has been erased from the agenda.
They take us for fools, I am not alone.
I am a ticking bomb. We can wait no longer.

One man, a man of destiny,
one man only need make his move. The rest will follow.
And they who have lied, the obfuscators, the collaborators,
those in denial, they will not be forgiven. They will be found.
They will be dragged from their homes and broken

till tarred and feathered and chained, in an ecstasy reborn,
in St Peter's Square, Wenceslas, Tiananmen
they will lead our exalted masses in one voice, one chorus
chanting the one almighty name:
Champion. Champion. Champion. The Wonder Horse.

Crimescene

The bear would say nothing.
Where the politician would have a prepared statement
or the disgraced celebrity a plea of *speak to my solicitor*,
the bear would say nothing;

nothing, that is, beyond the typical snuffling and grunting
you might expect from a worst-case down-and-out
or from an ex-prizefighter shambling and pitiful
with scrambled eggs for brains.

And this a ruse, some would say,
purely to evade the question.

But consider the short-sighted stare,
what lies behind it? Low intelligence
or a ponderous cunning, you can't be sure.
Or madness.

Coercion,
to get to the bottom of it for once and for all
is not possible with a bear.
No history of reasoning in his breed.

A friendly hug you dare not trust
lest inadvertently he go too far.
You would not choose to come between him
and the object of his lust.

A door, loose on its hinges, swings unpredictably in a
bear.
His past, a foggy yesterday, may never have existed
or two thousand years of tribulation
might gnaw at his conscience.

That they quit the region soon after, he and his tribe,
proves nothing. But note the massive shoulders,
the neck, the clamping jaws, the scooping paws, nails
fit to rip a tree easy as peeling a soft-skinned fruit.

Doubt and rumour, fable and religion.
What other creature would have strength
to roll aside a stone? Rob from a cave
the body of a man?

Sanctuary

Flashing lights out there, sirens racing past
are reduced to a blur and muted
through this pub window's etched and scalloped glass.

Trouble in the outside world.
Not here,

for I have coins in my pocket to jangle today.
Enough for a pint. And another and another,
a good few pints. Keep the world at bay.

went out for a haircut
fell down in the chip shop six hours later
how do you account for that

The Drink

It didn't take long, a short summer visit,
to pick up the habit while picking fruit,
strawberries in Somerset

and forty years on
I still put it to my head, just once in a while,
this loaded cloudy scrumpy-gun
to blow my cares away.

It's just it happens less often now
I wake on my back in a golden meadow
eager with a young man's thirst
to find out what might happen next.

So time now maybe for sober reflection,
to find a meaning if any,
that might lie behind what already has been;

to learn from all I've learnt in the past
and all the broken promises,
and I will, yes I will, so I will, believe me,
I'll begin after one more glass.

Crap Dad

He sang and he sang,
he sang throughout.

He sang while she chose a site.
He sang while she busied herself collecting materials
and attended to the nest-building.
He sang for the fourteen days she sat in incubation

and now, while she tires herself out dashing here and there
across the lawn collecting worms to feed the young,
he, the natty one, sings from his perch
in the candy-floss froth of pink cherry blossom.

Composition is all, his golden bill
tilted to the sun. With vigilance nil.

So when the butchering magpie
lurches into a flight made heavy
by the beakful of nestlings he carries away,
our garden blackbird, Oh what a stink he raises.

Gorgeous in his outrage,
flinging himself from branch to branch
in an apoplexy of warning shrieks:
Danger. Danger. Danger.

Too fucking late now cock,
you're stuffed.

Supreme songster, neglectful sire,
your genes will travel no further.
Fantastic voice, sodding useless.
Crap dad this garden blackbird.

The Girl

If I had a daughter called Lily
I would button up her red woollen coat.
I would tuck up her hood with the fur trim
so she'd be warm.

She would be chatty as children are,
holding my hand all the way home,
and there I would leave her, where she was safe,
while I went back to the pub

to drink and drink and drink
and drink until I was rotten.
So what might happen then
to Emily and her mum?

No wait a bit. That's not right,
I get confused, I've had a few.
It isn't Emily, is it, course not,
it's Lily isn't it. Lily. Lily.

As Time Goes by

1 Valentine

Yes, I think I like you,
I like you very much.
I think if we were rabbits
I'd like it in your hutch.

Yes, I think I like you,
I like you very much.
I wish that we were rabbits
and I was in your hutch.

2 Avowal

Three things I have,
three things to sustain me,
I have the words, the ale and thee.

If they should fail,
were I to lose but one of these and yet survive,
that man would be a stranger to me.

3 Seven Year

Never thought I'd be
unfaithful to thee.
Never thought I'd see
a rhino up a tree

but it's up there now,
top-most branch,
great hornèd beast,
yoohoo, yoohoo, waving to me.

Only a Farmer's Daughter

The family resemblance was there in her face
clear for all to see: she was the daughter of course
of the local farmer, a pig-breeder,
but oh what knockers.

I kissed her once one summer's night
under the willows
while the water rats went *plop* further down the brook.

I said,
Can you hear them… listen.
She wouldn't.

She was warm and soft, leaning to me
wearing perfume, drenched in it, so sickly sweet
I couldn't help but think of her father's fields
rank with docks and nettles and the stink of slurry,
it was shocking.

Our teeth banged together as we kissed,

and it was only because she was nice,
really, really, sort-of nice, somehow,
that I didn't try to unbutton her blouse
like the lads did say she'd let you.

It was terrible.
I wanted to so much
I thought it would destroy me.

Nipples like walnut-whips, said Tandy,
Eeee they're grand.

Ball-valve and Stop-cock

Skin the colour of moonlight, mossy-soft and yielding
was the plumber's daughter, Hilary Fielding.

He was a good man, one you could trust,
he'd always come out if you had a burst

and expert he was at every kind of pipe
with his blow-lamp, solder and flux.

And Hilary, in some ways, took after him
though she favoured a more modern approach,

with flexible couplings, down on the river bank,
Lord was she
gorgeous to squeeze.

So while he did the plumbing for our mums and dads,
she kept a flow at tremendous pressure
pulsing through us village lads.

Come the Revolution

stale scones
stale scones

take 'em to the bridge
take 'em to the river
take 'em to the bridge over the river

and bomb the swans
bomb the swans

hissing gaping bullyboy swans
doting on their own reflections

snooty swanky puffed-up galleons
they're big bad buggers non-egalitarian

time to be drastic
be iconoclastic

the river is for all of us
not for just the powerful that think they're gorgeous

so moorhen dabchick coot unite
get the swans do what's right

if you're out of luck
you'll hit a duck

but it's very very hard
to sink a mallard

with stale scones
rock buns

take 'em to the bridge
take 'em to the river
take 'em to the bridge over the river

and bomb the swans
bomb swans

Inadmissible Advice to the Young

Now isn't it the case that when you're a young man
you always wake up with a hard-on,
and if you're in a hurry it can get in the way
between you and the sink
as you brush your teeth in the morning but –

if you are not in a hurry –
if you are a student say, of the arts perhaps,
then you might have time to reflect on the difference
between the narrow plastic shaft of the toothbrush
and your own stiff cock, thick and generous,
which you take in your other hand

and back across the landing,
over the arctic lino barefoot,
you may pad back to your bedsit bed
where the girl lies sleeping

and forget Dr Drakakis.
Go hang his tutorial on Spencer's *Faerie Queen*,
for in your arms, cleaving to you, drowsy for love,
you hold an enchantress of your own.

And later, yes later, there will be time;
there will be time for study and duty
but today let it be for love and youth
to go dancing down the worried streets,
beyond mortgaged lives and market places
to city parks with wider skies. And wine. Wine aplenty,
laughter and tears, dreams and kisses then, enough for poetry.

When cherries are ripe they must be eaten.
So make no apology – sorry Dr Drakakis –
make no apology, but celebrate. Celebrate.
Consult an artist if in doubt, consult the poet.

Myrmecophaga Tridactyla* Triptych

1 At a Glance

Anteaters aren't very interesting.
They eat ants.
They have little by way of conversation.

An anteater, after it's been busy for a while eating ants,
might be overheard to say –
especially if it knows you're listening –

Well that's enough ants for now
but I might have a few more later.
I'll do the same tomorrow I expect, and the day after.

They have no sense of irony.
Ants are what engage them,
precious little else.

2 Conspiracist's Theory

You have to hand it to the anteaters:
ants are what engage them, precious little else
exactly what they want you to believe,

They don't take risks,
they don't make mistakes,
they have infiltrated every level of society.

They have judges in their pockets.
They own politicians, laboratories, armaments,
mining-rights in unstable countries.

Preoccupied and unassuming,
preferring the cover of darkness
for discreet high-echelon conveyancing.

But note the snout: the give-away, prehensile,
poke-anywhere snout. And the tongue,
ever ready to snake out,

to grab an ankle, slit a throat,
drag into cover
any who become too curious.

A journalist's body discovered in the wilderness,
chest ripped up, ribs snapped apart, as if by claws
strong enough, to rend, for instance

the concrete towers and bunkers of termites.
They who harbor suspicion
know better than to voice concern.

Poets blanch. My neck is on the line,
in the event of my disappearance…

3 Last Minutes of the Meeting

Deep in the scrubland,
long after the moths had stirred into flight,
a shadowy figure addresses the meeting.
With *Any other business* he brings it to a close.
One last item.

A lone vigilante,
monitored from the start.
Not worth buying off.
Unreliable. Unstable. He's been taken care of.

FOOTNOTE:

*Other anteaters are involved in only small acts of larceny and
chiselling and fall under a different jurisdiction.*

The Bicycle, Some Facts in a Nutshell, with Footnote (music by Canned Heat)

Sir Walter Raleigh, inventor of the famous bicycle
as every schoolboy knows, was a very chivalrous man:

he laid his bicycle down once, didn't he just, in a deep puddle
so Ann Boleyn[1] could hop across without getting her frock wet.

But as history became more popular and began to gather pace,
Disraeli invented gears which improved things a lot
and yet please note:

no matter how fast you may pedal with new technology
you are not allowed in the third lane of our modern motorway
system

which owes so much to the work of a kindly Dr Beeching,
the surgeon whose powders are still available in the shops today,
and legal,

unlike those moreish little pills that help you zip up big steep hills.
They are frowned upon as dangerous. And rightly so,
indeed one could do worse

than introduce the young to *Amphetamine Annie,*
that never-to-be-forgotten song of the sixties
with timely unrelenting chorus: 'Speed Kills'.

---

[1] or it could have been Marie-Antoinette.
Sir Walter, it is said, knew of all the best puddles for miles around where he
might loiter with his bicycle at the ready.
His spirit of enquiry, appetite and ardour insuppressible and boundless energy
made him a great lover of women – a slippery dream of two at a time, folklore
will have it, is how he invented the tandem.

Poor Old Bird

Never again, Miss Hawthorne said after Mister Whiskers died,
I'm eighty-seven, it wouldn't be right to get another,
it wouldn't be the same.
She only had her telly and the radio for company,
geraniums on the window sill to care for.

He was on his last legs, she said, *like me. Oh but I miss him*
with nobody to talk to this old house feels lonely.
Then Miss Hawthorne had a stroke of luck,
Miss Hawthorne adopted Joey.

FREE the card had said,
stuck in the window at Help the Aged.
FREE TO A GOOD HOME
BUDGERIGAR AND CAGE

and Joey settled in.

Who's a pretty boy then?
Who's a pretty boy then?
Who's a pretty boy then? Miss Hawthorne would say
while Joey listened.

Joey listened to everything.

He cocked his head,
he nibbled his cuttlefish, pecked his millet,
ruffled his feathers, swung on his perch.
He twittered and chirruped into his mirror,
rang his little bell, excreted neatly,
but Joey never said a word.

Who's a pretty boy then?
Who's a pretty boy then?
Who's a pretty boy then? Miss Hawthorne persevered.

Christmas came and Christmas went.
Joey said nothing
till Easter came,
and then on Easter Sunday morning

(after The Sunday Service broadcast live
from All Souls' Church Langham Place,
with a grilled tomato done just to her liking,
Miss Hawthorne's chest was seized with pain)

Joey spoke for the very first time:

The Lord is my Shepherd. he said,
Comprendez-vous jig-jig Madame?

Dropping her plate, dentures flying out,
Miss Hawthorne fell,
cracking her head on the kitchen table.

Help, cried Joey, *Miss Hawthorne's dying.*
Help, Help, cried Joey. *Miss Hawthorne's dead.*

On Wednesday night a hedgehog
came in through the cat flap to chew Miss Hawthorne's ear.
Joey was weak without water,
hardly aware of the crunching.

The hedgehog returned the following night
to lap up some tomato and take a piece of nose,
but Joey was no longer balanced on his perch.

On Friday morning, alerted by a neighbour,
Community Constable Graham came to lean his weight
authoritatively against the door. The Yale gave way,
he found her.

Graham on his phone reporting to the sergeant,
A body, yes,
an old lady, yes,
I believe, the resident.
Dead a few days I'd say Sarge,
some damage to the features.
The work I suspect of a rodent.

Graham, as instructed remaining at the scene:

There'll be a doctor, he thought, *forensics, a photographer.*
Graham, studying the details, looking for clues,
takes note of the cage and lying on its floor
a pathetic pile of powder blue feathers.

Graham, like many a policeman,
didn't have a great sense of humour,
nor was he a born detective.
Musing to himself, Graham reflected,
Natural causes, poor old bird. No foul play suspected.

Paterfamilias

A complicated man, a powerful figure,
he trimmed his mistress' pubic hair
twice a year; took it to Paris

where he had a man – a wigmaker
on La Rue Parnasse –
fashion it into the false moustache

which he would wear at the requiems –
memento vitae –
of elderly distant members of the family,

... and your great aunt Grace was the last he said,
of that generation. Buried this year on the first day of spring
but it was bitter up there I can tell you, at St Stephen's:
the wind off the moor cutting down like a razor
and curlews wailing. Blue clay clogging our boots.
The daffs all trampled. I felt for the dead.

In the lee of the chapel,
its one bell silent, the mourners gone,
he stood like a tombstone.

The rain turning to sleet,
its melt and tears seeping through the moustache,
wetting his lips. The taste of cold salt.

Wolverine

With the exception of your Aunty Kitty,
the Wolverine ounce for ounce
is the most ferocious creature known to man:

this according to my Uncle Frank
who'd been up to the Klondike in his youth
and knew a thing or two.

The Native Americans he said, *call it 'Carcajou'*
which in translation means 'Let us leave this place'
or 'Quick. Run like Fuck', depending on the circumstances.

It's a crazy fearless brute, he said,
wild enough to go for a full grown moose.

Aunty Kitty was a tackler down at the mill.
Eeee, she's mustard, said Grandma. *She's a Tartar.*

She stormed into the chip shop that night
next to the Lamb and Flag, she had a face like thunder,
she was seeing red as Blowsy Phyllis leaning over said,
I've a lovely haddock for you here, Frank.
I saved it for you special.

Frank screamed, *O Bejaysus!*
He threw down sixpence, grabbed his haddock
and made himself scarce in the time-honoured way
of all Algonquians facing such a menace.

Hot Licks

Recently bereaved Mad Uncle Daniel
dipping his balls in a jar of Bovril
said, *Oh how I miss her.*
I do miss that girl you know, your Aunty Avril.

Lovely hot tongue she had,
better than this spaniel,
but she was pedigree, convent and orphanage,
the pup's what I got from the small ads.

Loved her Bovril, your Aunty Avril.
But I'm training it up
and it's doing very nicely.
Here you are, pup, suppertime.

Blue Easter Hyacinths

The Creeping Rat-arsed Fuck-billed Piddler
long thought to be extinct,
last seen in the eighteen sixties in Samoa,
was rediscovered by my Granddad
breeding up on the moors beyond Todmorden.

It builds its nest out of factory chimneys,
broken cartwheels and railway sleepers,
is what he told my Grandma.
But it wasn't true.

He had no abiding interest in ornithology,
no, his heart belonged on Floss Ogden's barge,
a floating brothel with velvet curtains
on the Leeds–Liverpool canal.

And he proved courageous my granddad;
he saved three women when it went up in flames,
but Floss was lost. He was badly burned
and never the same thereafter.

So long ago, who would remember?
I mention it because the mysterious bowl of blue hyacinths
that appears on his grave each year at Easter
is there again now. I can show you.

Predator and Prey

1 Bobtail

This is a poem about rabbits,
once we called 'em coneys.

This is a poem about hutches
because that's what we call where rabbits live
unless they're out in the wild, tha knows,
in which case they live in warrens, in burrows,

in fear,
of snares
and dogs stoats cats weasels myxomatosis foxes eagles
ferrets nets guns and men.

But they're good at breeding,
they're good to eat
and it's not very long since I had one.

Little girl crying, hutch empty, door open,
she doesn't know where it's gone.
Bobtail...
Bobtail...

Ah,
the wolf, little girl, the wolf.
A creature I fear I neglected to mention.

2 Bushytail

Grow little chicken,
not quite ready yet
with enough young meat on.

Dry and tough the mother hen;
pay no heed to the old bird's clucking,
disregard that silly warning,

the corn is sweeter away from the farm,
the grubs fatter, the berries riper
here down the lane.

Oh,
how perfectly
delightful.

I'm sure we'll meet,
when I call again and I am,
I assure you…

(Red fur, handsome whiskers, bushy tail,
licking my …mmmm… licking my lips.
I do beg your pardon.)

Yes I am,
every inch, oh every inch, trust me,
a gentleman.

3 Tailtwister

He formed the Welfare Corps for Cats
because cats were what he hated most,

liked to have them round in plenty
all caged up nice and handy

so he could tweak their tails
when no-one was looking, tug their whiskers.

Anywhere you met him, his manners,
you'd consider him a gentleman,

but the cats knew better.
Mother cats would hiss a warning to their kittens,

If you're not good you know who'll come,
the Welfare Man,
he'll come and take you away.

To sympathetic visitors he'd say,
A splendid animal, yes I agree
but I don't recommend you adopt it.
The poor creature is very disturbed,
why even I must wear my gauntlets
before I attempt to approach it.

Oh how sad, they'd say. *So perhaps next time,*
but for now, please, do accept this small donation.
Such a kindly old man, they'd think.

But see him on a winter's day,
brisk and chipper, striding out,
fine soft linings to his shiny leather boots.
Snuggest fur in his mittens.

Or Her Sister

Oh how I adore and my heart aches
for the girl in the cake shop selling cakes,
and bread. White. Granary. Wholemeal. Decisions.
How can I tell her how I feel?

A day-old loaf is half price,
she'll slice it for you if you like,
it makes the nicest toast.

I like it with butter and honey
or dipped in my egg at breakfast.
Lightly boiled. Free-range is best.

She makes sandwiches so obligingly,
ham and mustard, egg and cress, cheese and chutney.
Always wears a spotless pinny. Heavenly meringues.
Oh I would pay a king's ransom…

A note in the window says
      FRESH FRUIT TARTS TODAY
      ARE RHUBARB, OR DAMSON.

A little bell above the door goes *tingggg*
ever so brightly as you walk in
but sometimes there's a queue.

What I'll say is:
I'd like a hot meat and potato pie, please.
Will you come out tonight with me?

What do you think, will she?
Or I might change my mind. Her sister's nice.
Vanilla slice. I might have a steak and kidney.

Glory Be

The slightest tilt, Dianne Hathaway,
of your breasts takes my breath away,

down the street so proudly walking
to the parish church on Sunday morning,

you are the vicar's wife and I'm sixteen
I follow bent double, y-fronts torqueing,

through the lychgate 'neath the ancient yews,
slim pretty ankles, high-heel shoes,

men long dead from under their stones
rise to her beauty rattling their bones.

Now from my pew in the meagre congregation
throbs in captivity my veneration

as she sings hymns by the stained glass window
I see her unveiling in translucent colour

and this I'll remember lathered in my bath:
moist lips, the pulse in her throat, her deep, red, open, mouth.

Kneeling at her feet with my tower of love
I lift up mine eyes to her heavens above

where to ease this awesome want
with manhood's baptism at her font

and all through the dire sermon, whip me, whip me,
I pray to the Lord with the devil of a hard-on,

so help me if she takes communion,
I dare not watch lest I come,

ejaculate in my Sunday best,
limp home in shame to mother's breakfast,

semen on my belly
drying to a crust.

'...the beat beat beat of the tom-tom'

After a few pints
down in the taproom of The Swan with Two Necks,
Peggy Lee put her hand on my knee.

(In such a hurry I'd been once,
turning to pursue her,
I reversed into a lamp-post and put a big dent in my bumper.)

We were sitting so close,
and as we spoke
she was stroking my leg just above the knee.

She knew damn well what it was doing to me
and all the while smiling sweet and innocent.
O, she give me fever.

True,
except it wasn't really Peggy Lee,
or Eartha Kitt either.

But Lord was she
a foxy lady.
O, she give me fever.

Nanuk

I said, *I'm an Eskimo.*
You said, *No,*
are you fuck,

you're one of Dick and Eileen Ackroyd's lads
from down Bermondsey Street
you're one of us.

And you loaded the dog-sleigh,
you harnessed the huskies,
you chiselled the runners free of ice

and crying, *Mush Mush*
you pulled away beneath the stars
and vanished in the darkness.

You took my heart
and you never looked back.
You took the harpoons, the sealskins, the eider duck

and it's cold in the igloo
now without you.
No one to hold,

no one to say,
Nanuk, you're lovely,
Nanuk, I love you

The Things That You're Li'ble

It's a poor workman blames his tools, I know they say that
but Bloody Hell, he said, *I ask you, look at the state of this lot.*

And it was true,
you never did see a pile of tools in such a sorry state:

the adze had had it, the set-square was anything but,
the scribe pointless, gimlet shot-at, the spirit level sunk very low.
The bradawl had lost its grip entirely, the clamps were clenched
and the saws only so-so, very very middling, a sad collection
disinclined to sink their teeth into anything;
chisels without edge, mallets drooping, a dismal plane,
a dubious brace with its bits all bent.

Well never mind, I said, *time's getting on.*
What do you think, should we get cracking?

He sighed, chose the brace, but it swung around
all unhinged and wonky in his hand.

Dammit! he said and he chucked it.
It flew like a broken heron. It landed in the sand.

I don't know how I got this job, he said, *I'm a goat-herd,*
served my time. My father was a goat-herd
and his father before him. I'm not a bloody carpenter
I'm a goat-herd.
How long have we got lad, what do you reckon?

Search me, I said, *but the sky's looking dark over yonder.*

This timber, he said, *it's green see, never been cured properly,*
all these boards are warped to buggery.
Tatty old rope for caulking. Tar like gnat's piss.

ARK he says to me, His Nibs from on High, just like that.
'Noah. Build an Ark'.
Oh Aye! Righty-ho then Lord, straightaway. No problem.

ARK – so what's a bleeding ark when it's at home?
We've never had Arks before.

44

And plans? Instructions? They might come in handy,
not that I could read them. What about you lad,
can you read? I shook my head.
O God, he said,

and from the sky there came a great rolling peal of thunder.
It upset all the animals queuing in pairs.
They roared and grunted, they howled and barked,
screeched, jibbered and trumpeted.

And you can all shut the fuck up with that bleating, yelled Noah.
It's only a bloody fairytale, nothing's going to happen.

But he pulled two planks together in a hurry,
took a mighty swing with the hammer.
Its head flew off, he hit his thumb,
I looked away.
I didn't say anything.
And the first fat blobs of rain began to fall.

Lay Preacher

A sparrow at the zoo, perky as you please,
went hopping along chirruping to the flamingos,
Prithee why so haughty?
Without long legs you wouldn't be so tall,
if your necks were shorter you'd be quite small.
And then what, d'you know,
you'd be silly pink ducks with daft bent bills
and that's all.

What we must do is examine ourselves,
take me for instance, look,
my garb is sober as a lay preacher
but if I had plumes – long crimson streamers spilling from my tail
or a crimson crest I could erect at will –
well then you might call me Passer Domesticus Superbus,
but I'd still be the cocky little fellow that I am,
down to earth, no airs and graces, inside
I'd still be the same.

I scattered some crumbs from a currant bun.
He flew to my feet, he hopped about,
disdainful of crumbs, considering.
And then in earnest began his chirruping.

Chirruping a list of my shortcomings,
chirruping, he dressed me down,
chirruping his list of my conceits,
my self-delusion, self deception,
chirruping, chirruping, on and on,
with his chirruping, chirruping, chirruping

until I'd had enough:
I chucked my bun at him
and fled.

The wily bird.
He got the bun he wanted.
But I'm wiser now and purged
as a preacher might've intended.

…and you can come too, too, too

I thought I'll go to the temple
I will I will
but on the way I met my pal
my pal the devil and his alcohol.

I thought I'll go to the temple
I will I will
but on the way I met my pal
my pal the devil with dope to sell.

I thought I'll go to the temple
I will I will
but on the way I met my pal
my pal the devil and a dancing girl.

So I went to the devil
again and again
now I'm walking past the temple
the door is open.

For James
(may his semen always stink like pelican shit)

If you've never been all that bothered
or fussy about religion then *Do as you would be done by*
seems a decent code to live by, it'll do for me,
plain and simple, a handy rule of thumb

because otherwise these ready-made prayers like
Forgive us our trespasses
as we forgive those who trespass against us
can present me with something of a problem,
specially when I think of James.

But I forgive James.
James the two-faced lying bastard
whose knackers should've shrivelled and dropped off by now
if my wishes have been granted.
May blackheads proliferate under his cock;
may his mouth always taste of where a dog's tongue goes,
but I forgive James.

I forgive James to such an extent
that whenever he tries it on again
gobbing-off with a pile of shite,
I'd like a scruffy old off-white miniature poodle
to appear at his feet, grab him by the calf and set to
fucking his ankle.

And it would not let go.
It would not be shaken off
until either he stopped being deceitful
or it had shot its load down his leg,
soaked his socks and given him a slippery shoeful.

James I forgive you,
whelks up your nostrils
stools of thistle and gorse entirely
caustic piss stingy as Dettol
rancid nob-end warty and fungal.

So thus endowed, James I forgive thee,
go with my two-finger blessing,
long may you live to a ripe old age
and here's to you… a toast… cheers… wishing you all the joy
of corns and verrucas, bunions, tapeworm,
gout, crabs, gripe, the jip, and haemorrhoids.

James repent.
You gave me your word,
we shook hands once, I bought you a pint
and I don't like being had.

Courage

The capercaillie is a giant grouse.
A capercaillie attacked a postman once
and knocked him off his bicycle in Scotland.

A rooster, a Rhode Island Red, a big bad sod
came at me once when I was six
and I had to run away.

But next time I was ready with a stick.
I caught it a right cracker on the head
and it wobbled off all bandy-legged.

Stanley Burquehart was a stinker.
He was the bully at our little school.
I wish I'd hit him with a stick,

or a hammer. On the head.
I wish I had. I wish I had.
I wish I'd had the courage.

Lost Boy

The air hung wet; it clung around us
hot on our faces as the breath of an animal
gone with fever.

Best we could
we toiled in the fields till the storm broke
then we ran for cover.

Louisa got a nosebleed.
We stood in the barn, nothing to say.
We watched the crops go to ruin.

Such times, I wonder where he could be,
our lost boy, Sugden, who broke, I guess,
and ran right out one night barefoot, naked

into the black crackling hell of a storm same as this.
Makes you wonder what we are pitted against.
He'd be twenty.

Rips the heart out of a family.
We try not to remember.
Try to avoid his name.

...unless in our oceans

Before the coming of the white man, wheelbarrows
wheelbarrows in their thousands tens of thousands
roamed these plains.

After the white man came, a little while later, it wasn't long after,
he grew tired of galloping and galloping,
galloping across the boundless plains.

He said, *What we want is the Iron Horse.*
The Iron Horse can span this distance. The Iron Horse
will rein it in. Best bring on the coolies.

So the coolies came but the coolies came with a problem.
The coolies who would do all the work, digging hardcore, fixing
tracks,
couldn't do the work fast enough

because their trousers were too slack. Their trousers
kept falling down. And this brought in the ruthless men,
ruthless men who would stop at nothing.

The ruthless men had a solution:
they waded into the wheelbarrow herds,
they cut a swathe through the wheelbarrow herds

upending wheelbarrows left and right
wrenching wheels off slashing tyres
to get at the precious inner tubes. Inner tubes only

were what they wanted, best price paid,
for rubber belts and rubber braces
keeping up the coolies' trousers,

so with both hands they could work harder, did work faster
laying down tracks for the Iron Horse that came up shunting
right behind them, snorting, belching smoke and fire

over the prairie barren and empty.
Empty save for sagebrush,
save for broken barrows bleached by sun,

broken barrows scoured by wind,
skeleton barrows,
skeleton perches for buzzards and crows.

Totemic herds lost and gone.
Lucky since our enlightenment,
it could never happen again…

Corbies

Three crows bent on villainy, ruffian crows,
veterans of skullduggery, strode the foreshore
poking here, stabbing there
while a freshening wind tugged at the bladder wrack.

Storm be a-brewing out yonder croaked one.
Boats might founder quoth another.
Let's say a prayer rasped the third.

He raised his bill,
he cocked his head,
he watched the women gather on the pier head.

O Great Almighty Crow, he said, *our Provider,*
Send us a fisherman fresh-drowned dead.

And let his hors d'oeuvres all be in place croaked one.
Don't let the crabs've scraped his face quoth the other.
Or them knackering gulls got his eyes rasped the third,

and the rest we'll share with raven and fox.
There'll be bones left a-plenty to comfort his widow,
to bury in the churchyard under a cross.

The women on the pier head prayed for their men
while the gale grew stronger yet. It tore at their shawls,
it hurled their prayers and those of the crows
far over the solicitous void.

Brilliant Career

Here you are then Fatso, I said, *get stuck in*
and I slaps the plate down in front of him right merrily.
Claridges. I was maître-d' but they sacked me.

Hey Donkey Sausages, Goat Nakker Gravy,
and what can I get you today, Madam? quips I.
She bought some fillet, a venison pie… she looked at me funny
and the butcher sacked me.

Go in Peace, I intoned, *You've said you're sorry,*
a bit of what you fancy does you good.
In Nomine Patris. *Cheers. Blimey!*
Does this wine taste of blood?
They threw me out of the priesthood.

But never mind. Roses are red,
the sky is blue, clouds are fleecy,
there's a job here going for a poet, bloody'ell,
I'll give it a whirl it might well suit me.

Sex and the Wheelbarrow

Not being all that smart or lively at thinking
I was never much good at what you might call
the Art of Conversation. Consequently I don't settle in
and I don't feel at ease at parties,

so I was just sort of standing there
surrounded by everybody on my own, in the kitchen at Zoe's
when a woman in the red dress turned to me,
... and what is it you do? she said, smiling nicely.

Well I was taken by surprise, but I didn't let it show,
I'm a gardener, I said. And remembering my manners –
it's polite to ask – *and what about you,* I said, *what do you do?*
She said, *I'm a sex therapist.*

Oh-my I said, *My-my. By Jove that's interesting,*
so you must be a really good fuck then.
There was a pause. She didn't say anything,
So I went on –

Well, you know, when I say I'm a gardener, what I mean is,
I'm not the sort of fellow who can graft your fruit trees,
bring a lovely bloom to your peaches up against a hothouse wall,
fettle your bromeliads, that sort of thing,
I'm more of a labourer you see, slash and burn,
I spend a lot of time digging and weeding,
going backwards and forwards with my wheelbarrow

and d'you know what, damn and blast it, it was only this morning
I got a flat tyre with a full load on among the viburnums.
It were touch and go I can tell you, a right tricky moment,
a ruddy great thorn from off of floribundas had...
er... had worked its way in...

but the woman in the red dress had gone.
Just goes to show, like I say,
I'm not very good at parties,
not too hot at the Art of Conversation.

Garden of Repose

Too late for the delphiniums –

so now it is not to avenge them
but rather to protect the lupins
I take my scissors out at dusk
and snip the slugs in half.

It's a task I grant you not lighthearted,
but it's no very big deal either.
They needn't be very sharp, Snip-Snip,
any old scissors will do.

Some slugs are black, some leopard-skin.
This bonny one, fat as a finger,
is golden tree-sap, ginger-umber. Snip.
Their guts all ooze the same.

A flick of the wrist sends them sailing away
far out of sight into the shrubbery.
No great fuss,
just the way it is:

unappetizing remains under the shrubbery –
some such or thereabouts –
one day will be me, Snip-Snip,
one day, Snip-Snip, you.

Miracle in the Park

In-and-Out Franky, The Lush and me hatched a plan,
but when In-and-Out Franky and the Lush stood up
they both fell down. *Dregsy,* they said,
it is up to you and you alone,
what you must do is go to Fast Eddie's off-licence
and nick another bottle of wine.

Well in a roundabout way I got to my feet with some success,
held a tree to steady my balance; there was only us,
so I took my nob out to have a piss, a precautionary piss,
a piss just in case. Clever, I thought, strategic,
lest my mission should take some time.

And In-and-Out Franky the while was saying
...so from your elevated position up there now Dregsy,
if you look to the north and west over the city,
you will see but two factory chimneys.
When I was a lad there were twenty.
Church spires still standing, eight. Am I right?
And all of them empty except for the one selling carpets.
Dwindling congregations don't surprise me a bit,
if they're still preaching the same old guff.
What I do regret though is any spiritual gap
should be filled with such celebrity shite. Blimey, when I...

How many, Lush butted in, *them factory chimneys,*
you know, how many were there, when you were a lad?

Oh never mind, said In-and-Out.
Dash it Lush, try to keep up. Anyhow,
off you go then now Dregsy, okay.
You'll have to let go of the tree. Good luck,
get anything you can except Martini.
And better do your flies up there. Good lad.

And so I set out, all very slanty, everything swimmy,
and then there came the miracle;
suddenly she was among us, Smash-hit Suzie,
Smash-hit Suzie come to save us,
with two great jugs of Somerset cider,
Smash-hit Suzie, one in each hand.

She was steaming already and spoiling for a fight
but while we had cider we should not worry,
it did not matter, it would be alright.
And wasn't she lovely. Isn't she lovely,
pulling no punches, swinging wild,
aiming low, our lovely Suzie.
Lovely. Lovely.

For Shirley

Mooncalf-looking
face like a motorway pile-up
but she went down well
where there wasn't much light
under the bridge by the Skinner's Arms
where it crosses the canal.

Stan has video.
Stan's her pimp.

It's strong, he'll tell you,
this'll get it twitching,
you'll be after shagging t'hamster's ass
through t'bars of its cage int' kitchen.
All tastes catered for,
yours for a tenner.

It shows her with, in this order,
a midget, a leather man, a nun with a dildo,
clotted cream, ping-pong balls
a bottle of Newcy Brown and a python.

Hope?
No girl, you never had any,
or marbles,

you never had a skipping rope
or any family that wouldn't sell you
for booze or dope
and slip you some;

nice little earner,
slag at ten,
sticky little fingers
in the pockets of men.

And that mostly was her schooling
but she'd wear a gymslip for you
if that's what you wanted,
you could tie her up if the money was right.
Anything.

The only time she'd laugh
was out of it, you'd see her
swaying on a barstool in the Skinner's with the alcys.

She'd cross and re-cross her legs like a lady,
cough through teeth like a worn old chainsaw's,
spit in a paper hanky.

If she caught you looking
and she didn't like you,
she'd give you a mouthful,
she had a foul mouth.

But that last time
under the bridge, she went down,
it wasn't on a punter,
she jumped underwater.

Nobody noticed.
Nobody missed her.

She came back up about a week later,
floating without heroin, the first time ever,
this lost woman, Eve's broken daughter,

buoyed up at last in death at least,
under the bridge in poor light,
not by a brother,
not by a sister,
by dark scummy cold canal water.

One for Sorrow

The sly magpie took note,
kept watch in March.

He paid his visits,
made good his escapes in April;
egg-yolk yellow his bill.

Blind new hatchlings,
pink as mince,
he carried away in May.

Only in June,
late-on for the songbirds' breeding season,
I winged the bugger with an old air gun

and I tracked him down.
Got him cornered in a hedge-bottom,
stamped on his skull even while he was cursing.

Left him unburied.
Black, white, bloody.
Carrion.

Tiggywinkle

I expect you'll have noticed
there haven't been many good poems about hedgehogs recently
so here's one.

Oops, I say though, hold on,
because no sooner has it got started
than it takes an unexpected turn
with the arrival of this bloke from Kwikfit

and his wife, who, when he's out at work,
is having it off with a baker from across the road.
And the baker's HIV positive
but nobody's told him yet.

It's his skin she loves,
it's just so smooth and silky.
Well it would be, she tells her pal,
working with all that flour…

Not like my Brian, she says,
when he comes home and I undress him
even his nob tastes of Duckhams.

Brian fitted a tyre this morning
and balanced the wheel
that is racing towards the hedgehog tonight.

And the driver isn't concentrating –
his mind's on something else –
he's in a hurry to meet a new lover, a baker.

It's too late to brake when he sees the hedgehog
and something's coming the other way.
It's enormous, it's an Eddie Stobart truck,

he'd like to swerve,
but there's no room to manoeuvre…o
…and our little urchin's out of luck.

So, there you are, see, like I said, easy,
poem about a hedgehog, piece of cake.

Odd One Out

I always was the odd one out
 – unusual among the lemmings –
so when they said, *Come on we're off.*
I said, *No, I'm not going.*

But you are one of us, they said,
you really have no choice,
because when you are a lemming
you must do as a lemming does,

and they swept me up.
They carried me off over the cliff
and down down down we fell
into the sea to drown.

Lemmings don't believe in poets.
I think I might have been one.
Never be a lemming
with no voice to call your own.

Big Brother Lite

Don't worry about the wallaby
being only small
when compared with the Big Red Kangaroo.

A Big Red Kangaroo wannabe
the wallaby
is not.

He hops about and gets around
without the prodigious leaps and bounds
of the Big Red Kangaroo

and with not one jot of envy.
An unusual marsupial,
the wallaby reasons:

Why even the Big Red Kangaroo
can only do
the things which he is able.

So thus untroubled,
free of anxiety
happy as can be with his lot is the wallaby.

And here he comes.
Oh look at him now, isn't he cute,
he's stopped to scratch his belly.

Introducing the Hippo

A man, any man I would think, or a woman of average stature, without undergoing any special training and one not suffering from back problems, ought to be able to manipulate over a short to medium distance on the flat, a wheelbarrow-full of stones and rubble that approximately overall is the size and weight of a hippo's head.

Quite a load, but the hippo's torso is a huge round silo.

The cartoonist, when he draws a desert island in the middle of the ocean has probably taken a hippo's belly as the source of his inspiration. He might plant a palm tree in the middle there to lend a sense of scale before he adds an amusing caption, often the wry remark of a drowning man. Ironic this if you consider how many drowning sailors, once washed up on a hippo's belly, have found the experience unsatisfactory and will later swear they wish they'd grasped at straws instead.

That said, however, the hippo, vegetarian and with his own kind gregarious, weighing in at a mighty 1000kg plus, is in general an immensely peace-loving species.

The baby hippo, about the size of a loaded wheelbarrow, is totally disarming. The parents, gentle and solicitous, teach their young all the dangers of skating on thin ice and alert them early to the possible malevolence of strangers – those who on safari might park up, wind a window down and say, *Would you like a lollipop? We're going to your Granny's, come on, hop in.*

When a hippo farts underwater crocodiles float to the surface stunned. A local in his dugout even miles downstream might be caught unawares by the shockwaves and heard to exclaim in Pidgin English or his native tongue *Oops, hey-up there, whoa, steady-on.* Now under normal circumstances you would never expect that fellow to be familiar with the origin of the hippo's name: *Hippos* from the Greek, Horse, and *Potamos*, River, for the hippo to him is less River Horse and more Giant Water Hog because a decent rasher of streaky could feed his whole family even at weekends when the in-laws came round.

If you look in his mouth when a hippo yawns you can see in the distance villages and towns.

But as regards man, the hippo on the whole, prefers to be shy and retiring. Nothing he likes more than to spend his day with the ancient sutras mumbled to himself *sotto voce* while he engages in meditative wallowing and thus, though figuring largely, he has kept a low profile since time began.

Many facts are not well known. Take the cruise liner for instance, you won't be aware of the hippo's role in its invention.

It was Noah long ago who suggested that because of cramped conditions on board, the hippos might like to swim alongside. The obliging hippos said, *Certainly. And if you'd care to throw us a rope we could tow you around a bit, it might help pass the time.*

Actually, this is really rather pleasant, Noah wrote in his diary.

And the idea was to catch on some years later among the well-heeled and elderly, while for the rest of us P&O, short for hippo, ply their ferries to this very day.

Why, even that very great book the Bible itself, before censors and editors got to work, was once liberally peppered with hippo-related incidents. Take Jonah for instance, his words no longer fully recorded after his spot of bother with the whale that time, well, you can imagine his annoyance when he fell into a hippo only two weeks later – a lot of bad Old Testament stuff about fatherless offspring and begetting came echoing forth from the cavernous depths of the hippo's belly. The hapless host on this occasion feeling queasy and tremendously embarrassed.

Another biblical gaffe, little known but no less shocking, occurred when Wossname, smiting with his staff and unaware of his precise location, declared, *On this rock I will build my Church... Oh fuck me it's moving!*

And so on, and so forth, I give you the hippo, a landmark species. We've hardly scratched the surface; this but a thumbnail sketch of an enormous canvas, but somewhere a line must be drawn. This presentation must come to an end, ladies and gentlemen, and so, kindly now return to your homes while remembering please to Mind the Gap, an uncommonly wide one on this occasion, for with characteristic reticence, and abashed by the prospect of tumultuous applause, our hippo has left the building.

Holydays and Washdays

Pegging out the washing
one worries so
which way up
the socks should go,

hung from the top
or the heel or the toe.
Mother didn't teach me,
I don't know.

They have to dry,
they're soaking wet
so some I hang this way,
some that. But mindfully:

for some would say
on certain days
one must certainly not
be pegging out the washing.

Is it true? Hindu, Christian,
Buddhist, Muslim, Jain, Druid, Jew, do tell,
as regards my socks,
what is the lore according to you